WE DRIVE
Oversize Loads

Ruby Tuesday Books

Alix Wood

Published in 2025 by Ruby Tuesday Books Ltd.

Copyright © 2025 Ruby Tuesday Books Ltd.

All rights reserved. No part of this publication may be reproduced in whole or in part, stored in any retrieval system, or transmitted in any form or by any means, electronic, mechanical, photocopying, recording, or otherwise, without written permission from the publisher.

Editors: Ruth Owen & Mark J. Sachner
Design & Production: Alix Wood

Photo credits:
Alamy: 15B (Taina Sohlman), 16T (Robert McGouey/Industry), 16B (Adwo), 17T (Peter Titmuss), 17B (Jim West), 19B (Rob Gray), 20 (Everett Collection Inc), 21 (JMF News); Shutterstock: Cover (Shooting it), 1 (Nuad Contributor), 3 (Pru Sanderson), 4 (Gilles Paire), 5 (Uwe Aranas), 6 (thelamephotographer), 7T (knelson20), 7B (fotografiko eugen), 8T (Vladimir Konstantinov), 8B (Tong_stocker), 9T (sky-lord), 9B (F Armstrong Photography), 10T (Antoni M Lubek), 11T (3D-Horse), 11B (vladdon), 12 (Thongchai.S), 13 (amophoto_au), 14B (vladdon), 15T (Andriy Blokhin), 18–19 (Rigucci), 22T (aappp), 22C (Joseph Sohm), 22B (Oleksiy Mark), 23T (Around the World), 23C (aappp), 23B (Vitpho); Alix Wood: 10B.

British Library Cataloguing in Publication Data (CIP) is available for this title.

ISBN 978-1-78856-589-9

Printed in Poland by L&C Printing Group

www.rubytuesdaybooks.com

Contents

How Do Trucks Deliver Giant Loads?..... 4

Glossary 22

Index... 24

How Do Trucks Deliver Giant Loads?

Truck drivers deliver all kinds of **cargo** every day.

Sometimes they must deliver an oversize **load** – such as a house!

An oversize load can be very wide, extra long, super tall or mega heavy.

A truck delivering a house

It takes lots of skill to transport an oversize load.

Before a driver delivers an oversize load, they must work out what **route** to take.

They check a map to look for narrow roads and tight bends.

Oversize load

A tight bend

They check for low or weak bridges and low overhead wires.

The truck driver may also check the route for dangers by driving it in a car.

Low overhead wires

A driver checks the truck's tyres before loading the cargo.

Tyre

The tyres must have plenty of air to carry a giant load.

Sometimes, oversize cargo is loaded onto a truck by crane.

The driver uses thick chains to make sure the load is secure and won't fall off.

Some **trailers** can stretch to help carry long loads!

The driver unlocks a pin and pulls the trailer to make it longer.

Some trailers can drop down to the ground to make them easier to load.

The trailer is lower than the wheels.

A low trailer also helps the driver fit a tall load under low bridges.

Sometimes a huge oversize load is moved by a giant trailer called an SPMT.

An oil rig on an SPMT

Wheels

An SPMT is made by joining together lots of trailer-like sections with wheels.

SPMT stands for Self-Propelled Modular Transporter. It can be the size of a football pitch!

The driver uses a remote control to steer an SPMT and make it move or stop.

An SPMT moving a road bridge

Each wheel can be turned, lifted or lowered into a different position from the wheels around it.

Oversize load drivers must show other vehicles that they are carrying an extra wide or long load.

Oversize loads have **warning signs** on the front, back and sides of the truck.

Warning signs

Drivers put red or orange flags on the load.

Flags

OVERSIZE LOAD

Oversize load trucks may have flashing lights to tell other drivers – giant load coming through!

An oversize load truck may have escort vehicles.

Escort vehicle

The escort might drive in front of the truck to warn drivers coming the other way.

This car has pulled over to let the truck pass.

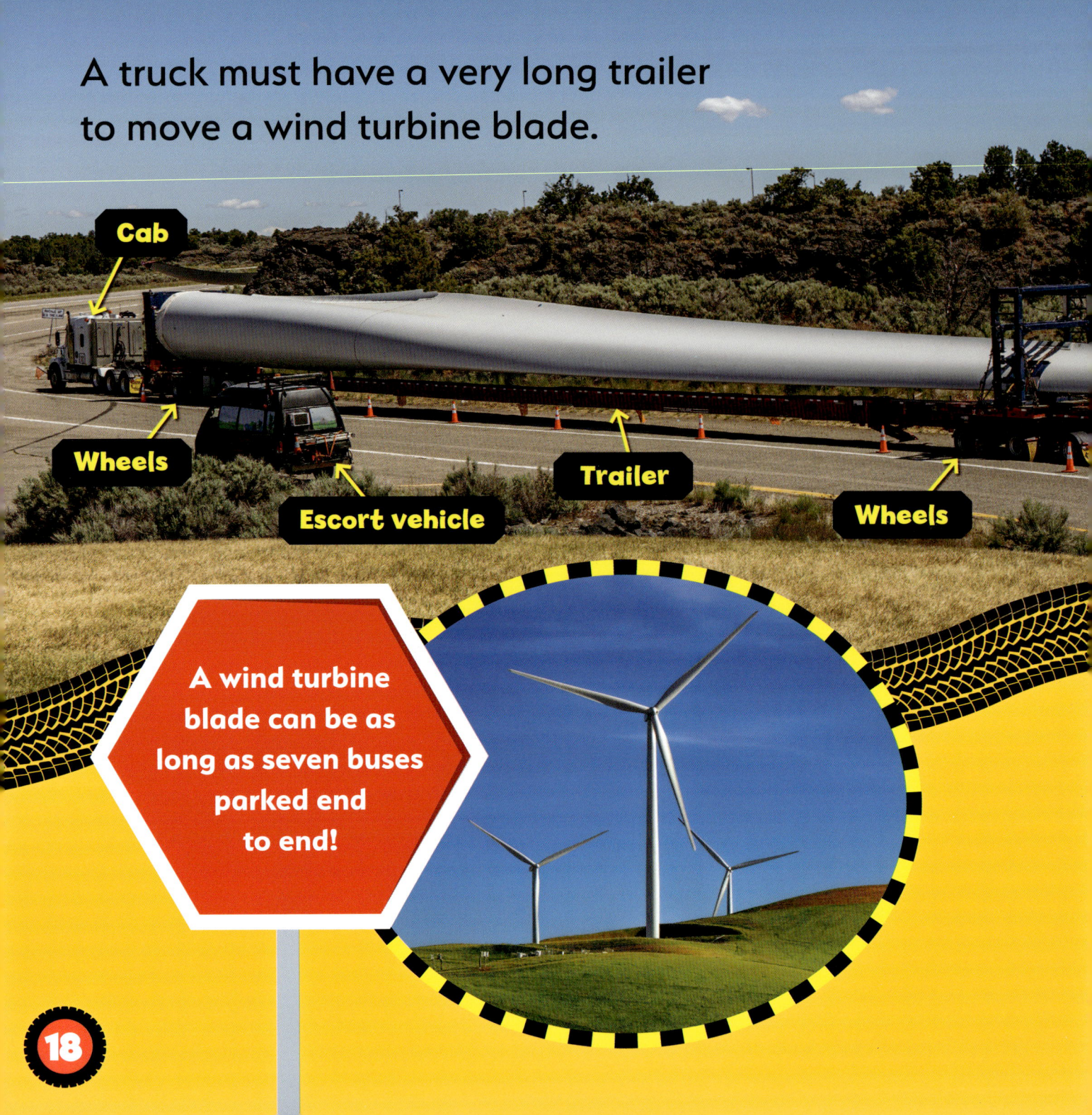

A truck must have a very long trailer to move a wind turbine blade.

Cab

Wheels

Escort vehicle

Trailer

Wheels

A wind turbine blade can be as long as seven buses parked end to end!

Blade

Blade

Blade-lifting machine

Sometimes a blade is too long to travel through a small town.

A machine on the truck lifts the blade up.

A driver must drive an oversize load very slowly and very carefully.

In 2012, a giant rock, which was part of an artwork, was moved in the United States.

The truck carrying the rock moved so slowly, it had to travel at night to stop it holding up daytime traffic.

Rock

The truck had 196 wheels.

In 2013, a giant part of an electricity power station, called a transformer, was moved in the United Kingdom.

The transformer weighed as much as 100 elephants!

The truck crawled along at 6.5 km per hour.

Every day, oversize load drivers are busy delivering HUGE loads!

Glossary

cargo
Goods that are collected and delivered by trucks, trains, planes or ships.

load
The objects being carried by a truck. Also the word for putting goods onto a truck.

route
The roads taken to get from one place to another.

secure
Safe and not in danger of falling.

trailer
The part of a truck that carries the load.

warning
A sign or message that tells people there could be danger.

Index

C
cargo 4–5, 8–9, 18–19
cranes 9

D
dangers (for oversize loads) 6–7, 16–17

E
escort vehicles 16–17, 18

L
loading cargo 9, 11

R
routes 6–7

S
SPMTs (Self-Propelled Modular Transporters) 12–13

T
trailers 10–11, 12–13, 18
tyres and wheels 8, 11, 12–13, 18, 20

W
warning signs 14–15
wind turbine blades 18–19